WINSTON CHURCHILL'S LONDON AT WAR WALK

Follow In The Footsteps Of Britain's Great World War II Prime Minister – Through London's Historic Westminster and St James's Areas

Paul Garner

WINSTON CHURCHILL

1874–1899

1874: (**30 Nov.**) Winston Churchill born at Blenheim Palace, Oxfordshire.

1888–1892: Attends Harrow School.

1893–1894: Attends and graduates from the Royal Military College at Sandhurst.

1895: (**24 Jan.**) Lord Randolph Churchill dies.

(**20 Feb.**) Commissioned into the 4th Hussars, a cavalry regiment of the British Army.

(**3 July**) Mrs Everest, Churchill's nanny, dies.

(**Nov.-Dec.**) Visits the USA and then travels to Cuba, where he begins his career as a journalist.

1896–1899: Military service in Egypt, India and Sudan.

During this period, Churchill's first book is published.

Fails to be elected as the Member of Parliament (MP) for Oldham and works as a War Correspondent for a daily newspaper. While reporting on the Boer War in South Africa, he is taken prisoner by the Boers while on a scouting expedition. He makes headlines when he escapes.

1900–1918

1900: Elected into Parliament as a Conservative MP for Oldham.

1904: Leaves the Conservative Party and joins the Liberal Party.

1905: (**9 Dec.**) Appointed Under Secretary of State for the Colonies (until 1908).

1906: (**2 Jan.**) Churchill's two-volume biography of his father is published.

(**13 Jan.**) Elected MP for Manchester, Northwest, for the Liberals.

1908: (**12 Sept.**) Marries Clementine Hozier at St Margaret's Church, Westminster.

1910: (**14 Feb.**) Appointed Home Secretary (until 1911).

1911: Appointed First Lord of the Admiralty (until 1915).

1913: Starts flying lessons.

1914: (**4 Aug.**) WWI begins.

1915: (**Feb.**) Helps orchestrate and plan the disastrous Dardanelles naval campaign and military landings on Gallipoli.

(**25 May**) Following the failure of these operations, Churchill is demoted.

(**June**) While at Hoe Farm in Surrey, he takes up painting.

(**11 Nov.**) Resigns from the Government. Joins the Army and goes to France to serve on the Western Front.

1916: (**8 May**) After six months' service in the trenches, returns to Britain to resume his political career.

1917: (**17 July**) Appointed Minister of Munitions (until 1919).

1918: (**11 Nov.**) WWI ends (Armistice Day).

TIMELINE

1919:	(**9 Jan.**) Appointed Secretary of State for War and Air (until 1921).
1921:	(**13 Feb.**) Appointed Secretary of State for the Colonies (until 1922).
	(**29 June**) Lady Randolph Churchill dies.
	(**6 Dec.**) Churchill is one of the signatories of the Anglo-Irish treaty.
1924:	(**6 Nov.**) Appointed Chancellor of the Exchequer (until 1929).
1925:	Formally rejoins the Conservative Party (after a period of 20 years).
1933:	(**7 Nov.**) Warns in the Commons that Germany has already begun to rearm.
1936:	(**Nov.-Dec.**) Incurs great unpopularity for supporting King Edward VIII during the Abdication Crisis.
1937:	(**12 May**) Coronation of King George VI.
1939:	(**3 Sept.**) WWII begins.
	Appointed First Lord of the Admiralty (for a second time) (until 1940).
1940:	(**10 May**) Neville Chamberlain resigns. Churchill is appointed Prime Minister and Minister of Defence (until 1945). He forms a coalition Government.
	(**9 Oct.**) Accepts the leadership of the Conservative Party.
1945:	(**8 May**) Victory in Europe (VE) Day.
	(**July**) Defeated in General Election.
	(**1 Sept.**) WWII ends.
1947:	(**3 May**) Two of Churchill's paintings (submitted in an assumed name) exhibited at the Royal Academy.
1951:	(**25 Oct.**) Appointed Prime Minister for a second term (until 1955) and Minister of Defence (until 1952).
1952:	(**6 Feb.**) King George VI dies.
1953:	(**2 June**) Coronation of Queen Elizabeth II.
	(**23 June**) Churchill suffers a serious stroke.
	(**15 Oct.**) Awarded the Nobel Prize for Literature.
1955:	(**5 April**) At the age of eighty, Churchill resigns as Prime Minister.
1963:	(**9 April**) Is made an honorary American citizen.
1964:	(**27 July**) Attends the House of Commons for the last time.
	(**15 Oct.**) Does not stand as a candidate at the General Election and steps down as an MP.
	(**30 Nov.**) Makes his last public appearance at the window of No. 28 Hyde Park Gate on his 90th birthday.
1965:	(**24 Jan.**) Dies in London at the age of 90.
	(**27-30 Jan.**) Churchill's body lies in state at Westminster Hall.
	(**30 Jan.**) A state funeral for Churchill is held at St. Paul's Cathedral.

1919 - 1965

ABOUT THIS WALK

This guided Walk starts on the steps of St Martin-in-the-Fields Church, which is easily found at the corner of Trafalgar Square, near the National Portrait Gallery. This Walk is split into two separate Stages (each with its own Map), which can be taken altogether or at different times if wished. Just follow the Directions and the route on the Maps, and read the information at each numbered stop.

Look out for Blue Plaques, Green Plaques and information boards en route, particularly those found on Statues, as they can give even more information.

*There are public toilets situated in Trafalgar Square and at Green Park Underground Station (**55**).*

16

The Churchill Statue
Created by Ivor Roberts-Jones, this Statue in Parliament Square, was unveiled by Clementine, Churchill's wife, on 1st November 1973, eight years after Winston's death.

FURTHER INFORMATION FOR THIS WALK

Please note that times are given as a guide only.

St Martin-in-the-Fields Church (1)
http://www.stmartin-in-the-fields.org/church
Tel: 020 7766 1100
Generally open throughout the day. See website for daily concerts and services.

Red Lion Public House (14)
http://www.redlionwestminster.co.uk
Tel: 020 7930 5826
Open: Mon-Fri: 08:00-23:00; Sat.: 08:00-21:00; Sun. 09:00-21:00

Houses of Parliament (18)
http://www.parliament.uk/visiting
There are a number of ways UK residents and overseas visitors can visit the Houses of Parliament including taking tours and watching debates and committees. See website for details.

Westminster Hall (19)
http://www.parliament.uk/about/living-heritage/building/palace/westminsterhall
See website for details of how you can visit.

St Margaret's Church (20)
http://www.westminster-abbey.org/st-margarets-church
Tel: 020 7222 5152 or 020 7654 4840 (Vestry)

Westminster Abbey (21)
http://www.westminster-abbey.org/home
Tel: 020 7222 5152
Open: to visitors from Mon.-Sat. throughout the year. Entry charge. Open: for worship only on Sun. and religious holidays such as Easter and Christmas. All are welcome and it is free to attend services.

The Westminster Arms Public House (24)
http://www.shepherdneame.co.uk/pubs/london/westminster-arms
Tel: 020 7222 8520
Open: Mon-Sat: 11:00-23:00; Sun: 12:00-22:30

The Churchill War Rooms (25)
http://www.iwm.org.uk/visits/churchill-war-rooms
Tel: 020 7930 6961
Open Daily: 09:30– 18:00. Charge

MAP NO. 1

KEY

1. St Martin-in-the-Fields Church
2. The Grand
3. The Corinthia Hotel London
4. The National Liberal Club
5. The Royal Tank Regiment Memorial Statue
6. The Royal Horseguards Hotel
7. The Old War Office Building
8. The Ministry of Defence
9. The Royal Air Force Memorial
10. The Battle of Britain Memorial
11. The Monument to the Women of WWII
12. No. 10 Downing Street
13. The Cenotaph
14. The Red Lion Public House
15. The Ministry of Health – Balcony
16. The Churchill Statue
17. Big Ben
18. The Palace of Westminster
19. Westminster Hall
20. St Margaret's Church
21. Westminster Abbey
22. No. 1 Sanctuary Buildings
23. The Methodist Central Hall
24. The Westminster Arms Public House
25. The Churchill War Rooms and Annexe
26. Admiralty House
27. The Admiralty Citadel
28. The Mall
29. The Duke of York Steps

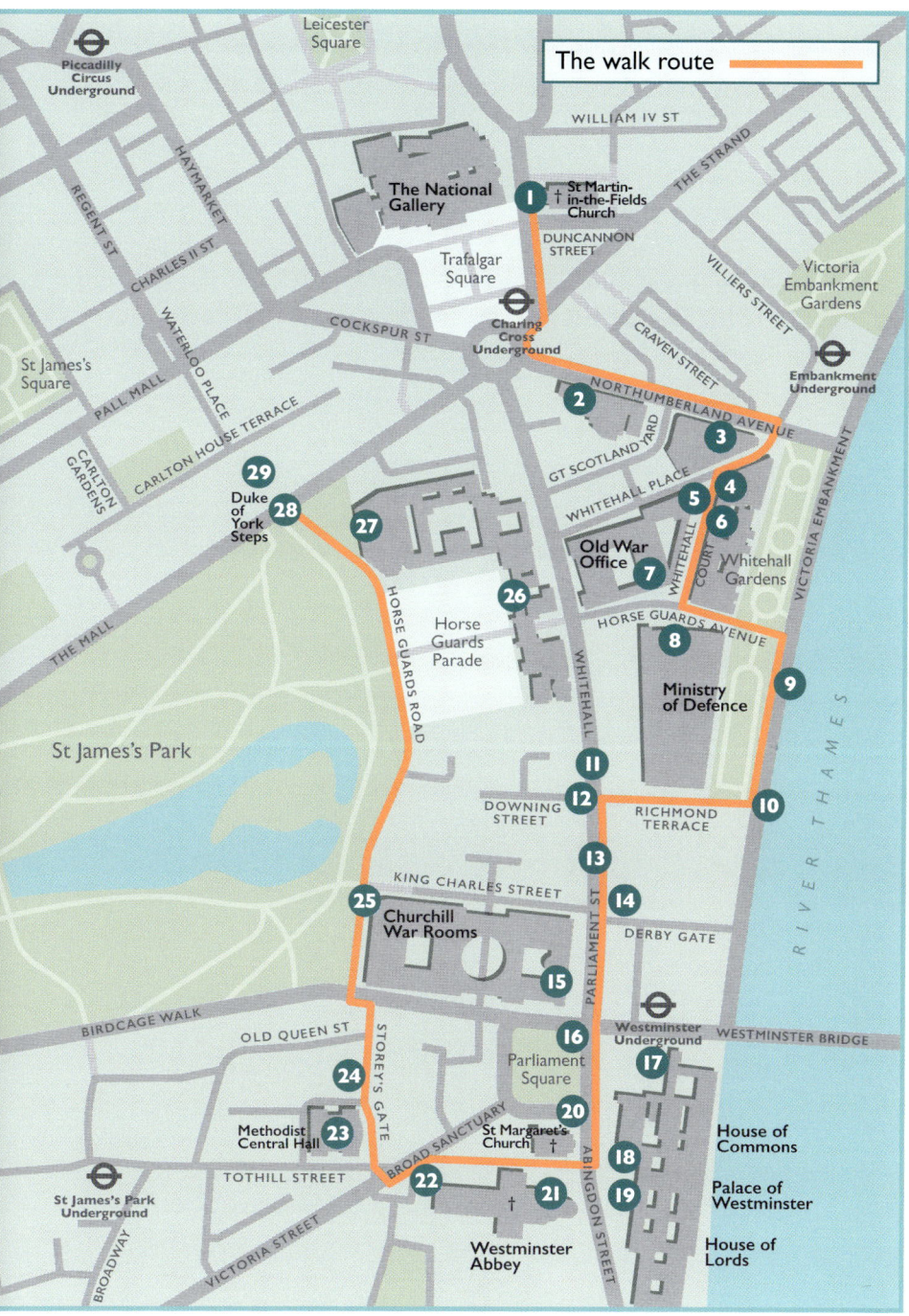

START OF STAGE NO. 1

Please Use Map No. 1

Directions: *To St Martin-in-the-Fields Church (1)*
From Charing Cross Underground Station: *Exit the ticket barriers, turn left and exit the Station via the stairs at Exit No. 7 ("St Martin-in-the-Fields" Exit). At street level, continue directly ahead to the steps of St Martin-in-the-Fields (1).*

From Embankment Underground Station: *Exit the ticket barriers, and turn left and walk up to the end of Villiers Street. Cross The Strand at the traffic lights directly ahead. Turn left once on the other side of the road, then turn first right and continue up Duncannon Street, with St Martin-in-the-Fields Church (1) further along on the right.*

1 ST MARTIN-IN-THE-FIELDS CHURCH

The Church's Crypt, which today is a café, was capable of sheltering hundreds of people and was used as an air-raid shelter in both World Wars.

During WWII, the US War Correspondent, Ed Murrow, bravely roamed the London streets broadcasting eyewitness accounts of how the War was affecting the City. His regular radio broadcasts, which each began with the words "*This is London*", were followed by millions of listeners in the USA.

At 11.30 pm, on 24th August 1940, Murrow famously stood on the steps of this Church, for one of his first reports. As air raid sirens blared in the background, he described, in vivid detail, the unfolding drama around him:

The searchlights, "*Lord Nelson on top of that big column*", the buses ("*double deckers*" - "*In this blackness, it [the bus] looks very much like a ship that's passing in the night and you just see the portholes*") and the eerie sound of people's footsteps "*like ghosts shod with steel shoes*".

Churchill realised the propaganda value of Murrow's live radio broadcasts to the American public.

So, he allowed Murrow access to London's rooftops, so he could record the sounds of bombs dropping, anti-aircraft fire and sirens. Although this helped sway American opinion in favour of Britain, it was the Japanese attack on Pearl Harbour in 1941, which finally caused the USA to enter the War.

Every year since 1947, a Christmas tree (usually a 50 to 60-year old Norwegian spruce, over 20 m tall), adorns the centre of Trafalgar Square. Decorated with 500 white lights, the tree is an annual gift to the people of London from the City of Oslo, as a token of gratitude from Norway to Great Britain for British support of Norway during WWII.

Note: as you pass Charing Cross Underground Station, on your right - that during WWII, this Station was known as Trafalgar Square Underground Station. This Station was directly hit by a bomb on the night of 12th October 1940, during the Blitz. The bomb pierced the ground and entered the Station below, exploding at the top of the escalators, 7 people were killed and 33 were injured.

Directions: *Following the Map, walk past Trafalgar Square, keeping it on your right, and enter Northumberland Avenue, which is the third turning on the left. On the right at No. 8, is a hotel called The Grand (**2**).*

THE GRAND (THE HOTEL VICTORIA)

This building was originally The Hotel Victoria, later renamed as Northumberland House, and is now a hotel called The Grand.

The Hotel Victoria, a 500-bedroom grand hotel built in 1887, was taken over by the Government during both World Wars. In WWII this building was used by Section 'F' of the SOE (Special Operations Executive).

In 1940, when the new Vichy Regime Government in occupied France signed an armistice with Nazi Germany, the British Government decided to set up a new secret fighting force. Churchill appointed Hugh Dalton to set up the Special Operations Executive (SOE), which became known as "Churchill's Secret Army". The SOE was to use non-military means to conduct espionage, sabotage and reconnaissance in all enemy and enemy-occupied countries, and to help local resistance groups. Churchill ordered that this "*army of shadows*" should "*set Europe ablaze*".

SOE's "F" Section was one of the sections concerned with operations in France. Its activities included disrupting Nazi operations and helping to supply, train and coordinate French Resistance groups in anticipation for the D-Day landings. "F" Section used this Hotel for recruiting agents. Room 238, which was used for interviewing candidates and assessing their motivation and character, is said to have contained only two chairs, a table and an empty filing cabinet.

Between May 1941 and August 1944, over 400 "F" Section agents were sent into occupied France. This number included 39 women – for in April 1942, despite opposition from some, Winston Churchill had given his approval for women in the SOE to be sent into Europe. It was dangerous work: the life expectancy of an SOE wireless operator in occupied France was only six weeks. Over 100 of these agents, including at least 13 women, lost their lives. Violette Szabo (codenamed "Louise"), whose story was told in the 1958 film "Carve Her Name With Pride' and Noor Inayat Khan (codenamed "Madeleine" and "Nora Baker") were two female "F" Section agents, who were executed (by being shot) by the Nazi's.

Directions: *The next hotel further along at No. 10 Northumberland Avenue is the Corinthia Hotel London (**3**)*

3 THE CORINTHIA HOTEL LONDON (THE HOTEL METROPOLE)

Originally built as the Hotel Metropole, in WWI, the Hotel was used as the Headquarters of the newly created Ministry of Munitions, "*charged with organising the supply of munitions of war*". In July 1917, Churchill was made Minister of Munitions and it was here that he worked and spent many nights.

The bow window of the Minister's room can be seen from the street in which you are now standing. Churchill stood looking out of this window on 11th November 1918, as he waited for the deadline set for the end of WWI (Armistice Day). The time for the ceasefire was 11.00 am in the morning. When the first stroke of Big Ben (**17**) rang out, Churchill recalled:

> *I looked at the broad street beneath me. It was deserted. .... another stroke of Big Ben resounded. Then from all sides, men and women came scurrying into the street. Northumberland Avenue was now crowded with people in hundreds, nay thousands, rushing hither and thither in a frantic manner, shouting and screaming with joy. ... Around me in our very headquarters, in the Hotel Metropole, disorder had broken out. Doors banged. Feet clattered down corridors. Everyone rose from the desk and cast aside pen and paper. All bounds were broken. ...* (The World Crisis)

During WWII, the Hotel was taken over by the War Office (see (**7**)) and used by its new department, MI9 which had its headquarters in Room 424. The activities of MI9 included supplying training about escape and evasion techniques to Allied servicemen (over half a million British people received this training during WWII), as well as helping to recover those who had become stranded behind enemy lines and providing escape aids to British Prisoners of War in German camps.

At the Hotel Metropole, Intelligence Officer, Christopher Clayton Hutton invented many of the escape aids, for which MI9 became well known (e.g., compasses that were hidden in buttons or fountain pens; and hacksaws, which could be concealed in a trouser-leg). Hutton is also credited with inventing cloth maps, which would not rustle or fall apart and which could be hidden in very small places. Escape aids helped prisoners to escape from Colditz Castle.

In November 2011, in an acknowledgement of the past history of this building, the official announcement of the "James Bond" film "Skyfall" was made at a Press Conference at the Corinthia Hotel London

 Directions: *Continue and turn right into Whitehall Place. Continue and take the first left into Whitehall Court. Immediately on the corner, at No. 1 Whitehall Court, is the entrance to the National Liberal Club (**4**)*

NATIONAL LIBERAL CLUB   4

Whitehall Court was built during the 1880s. Housed within this building is the National Liberal Club, established in 1882 by William Gladstone as a club providing facilities for Liberal Party campaigners. Churchill was a member of the National Liberal Club for 18 years and he would have used this Entrance.

Churchill was first elected to Parliament in 1900, as a Conservative, taking his seat in the House of Commons in February 1901. However, after just

four years, he joined the Liberal Party. As a Liberal, he was made Home Secretary in 1910. After being defeated in the 1922 election, Churchill left the Liberal Party, and later re-joined the Conservative Party; he famously said about this: "*anyone can rat, but it takes a certain amount of ingenuity to re-rat*". In 1924, Churchill was appointed Chancellor of the Exchequer.

A portrait of the young Churchill, as First Lord of the Admiralty in 1915, hangs inside the lobby of the building. The painting spent many years in the Club's cellar, due to splits within the Liberal Party resulting in Churchill being out of favour at the Club and then because Churchill defected to the Conservative Party. When Churchill became Prime Minister in May 1940, the Club put the painting on display in the lobby (as today). However, a year later, the painting was badly damaged (receiving a diagonal gash down its middle) during the Blitz when the Club suffered a direct hit. The painting was painstakingly restored and Churchill re-unveiled it himself in July 1943.

 Directions: *On the opposite side of the road is the Royal Tank Regiment Memorial Statue (5).*

THE ROYAL TANK REGIMENT MEMORIAL STATUE

The Royal Tank Regiment (RTR) is the oldest tank regiment in the world, formed in 1916, shortly after the invention of the tank. The Statue depicts the five-man crew of a WWII Comet tank and shows the unique comradeship which exists among the men who fight in tanks.

In 1915, Churchill held the position of First Lord of the Admiralty; the Admiralty was the organisation responsible for the command of the Royal Navy. Churchill, who had earlier learned about the idea of an armoured tractor, set up the Landships Committee to sponsor experiments and tests on these armoured tractors or "landships" as they were called. The development of these vehicles was so top secret that workers were told they were working on water carriers. People began to refer to them as "water tanks" and then "tanks" for short and that is how the vehicles became to be known as "tanks".

The first completed tank prototype in history, unveiled in the autumn of 1915, was called "Little Willie" (said to be an uncomplimentary nickname for the

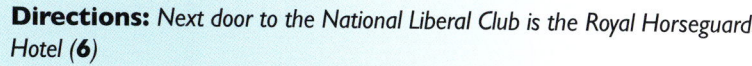

German Imperial Crown Prince Wilhelm). Although Little Willie never saw combat, it was a major step forward in military technology. A new prototype, known as Big Willie (named after the Crown Prince's father, Emperor Wilhelm II) was then constructed, which was to become the prototype for all British heavy tanks in WWI. The British were the first to use tanks on the battlefield in the Battle of Flers-Courcelette (part of the Battle of the Somme) on 15 September 1916. Although many of the tanks broke down, nearly a third were able to break through to the German lines.

When Churchill was Minister of Munitions (see (**3**)), he pushed forward production of the new tanks.

Directions: *Next door to the National Liberal Club is the Royal Horseguards Hotel (**6**)*

ROYAL HORSEGUARDS HOTEL

This Hotel is also situated within Whitehall Court. During both World Wars, the building was taken over by the Government and used by MI5 and MI6. Parts of the building also acted as Embassies for the USA and the Soviet Union during WWII.

Directions: *Walk down Whitehall Court and notice the large building which takes up the entire right hand side of the road, and extends as far as Whitehall. This is the Old War Office Building (**7**).*

THE OLD WAR OFFICE BUILDING

The War Office was the Department of the British Government responsible for the British Army, from the 17th Century until 1964. From 1906, the Department was based in this huge building, which has over 1,100 rooms on seven floors and 2.5 miles of corridors.

On 23 August 1909, MI5 was set up here (then called MO5), to tackle concerns about German spies in the country. It only had one member of staff, Captain Vernon Kell, who was known as "K". By the end of WWI, MI5 had a staff of about 850. Churchill did not have a good relationship with Kell, and one of Churchill's earliest actions as Prime Minister, in early 1940, was to dismiss Kell.

T. E. Lawrence ("Lawrence of Arabia") worked here, in 1914, at the outbreak of WWI, helping the Geographical Section with maps of the Middle East. Lawrence later became an Adviser to Churchill on Arab Affairs when Churchill was appointed Colonial Secretary in 1921. Lawrence also became a personal friend of the Churchills and was invited to their house-parties.

In March 2016, the entire Old War Office building was sold on a long lease arrangement to the Hinduja Group in partnership with OHL Developments for a price in excess of £350 million. The building will be sympathetically restored and redeveloped as a high quality hotel, and residential apartments.

 Directions: *Continue to the end of Whitehall Court and directly opposite is the modern day Ministry of Defence (**8**).*

THE MINISTRY OF DEFENCE

Today, this building is part of the Ministry of Defence, into which the War Office was incorporated in 1964.

Underneath the building is the secret Pindar Bunker. Originally conceived in 1980, with work starting in 1984, Pindar was finally completed ten years later at a cost of over £126 million. The Bunker's purpose is to provide a protected operations centre for the Government in civil emergencies and in the event of an enemy attack.

Directions: *Turn left into Horse Guards Avenue and walk to the end. Cross the road at a safe place and turn right, and on the other side, 25 m along, is the Royal Air Force Memorial (**9**)*

THE ROYAL AIR FORCE MEMORIAL　**9**

This Memorial was unveiled in July 1923, by the Prince of Wales (later King Edward VIII), originally commemorating the casualties of the Royal Air Force (RAF) during WWI. In 1946, additional inscriptions were added in memory of those who died in WWII.

The gilded eagle at the top of the Memorial is taken from the badge of the RAF, and looks south towards France. Around the top of the pillar are the words "PER ARDUA AD ASTRA", which is the motto of the RAF meaning "through adversity to the stars".

On 15th September every year, a wreath is placed at the foot of the Memorial to commemorate Battle of Britain Day.

[The Church of the RAF is **St Clement Danes Church**, which is situated on the Strand (not on this Walk). Inside the Church, gifts and memorials from individuals, organisations, and air forces from around the world, reflect this role. The floor of the nave and aisles is inlaid with around 1,000 slate squadron and unit badges and below the aisle windows are the RAF rolls of honour. Outside the Church are Statues of two of the RAF's WWII leaders – Air Chief Marshal Sir Hugh Dowding and Sir Arthur "Bomber" Harris.]

Directions: *Continue along the Embankment to the Battle of Britain Monument (**10**).*

THE BATTLE OF BRITAIN MONUMENT

The Battle of Britain, was a WWII combat, which took place from July to October 1940, when the RAF (headed by Sir Hugh Dowding's Fighter Command) defended the United Kingdom against the attacks of the German Air Force (the Luftwaffe – headed by Hermann Goering). The Luftwaffe waged a campaign, in which they

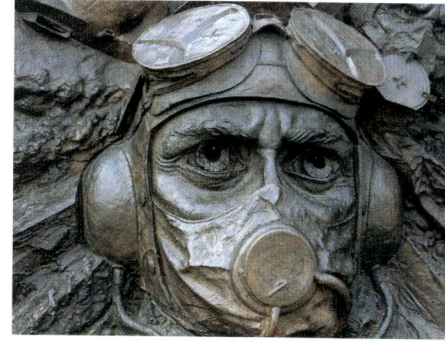

attempted to destroy the RAF in the air and on land and to gain air superiority, in preparation for a seaborne and airborne invasion of Britain. The name of the Battle stems from Churchill's historic "Finest Hour" speech given in the House of Commons (**18**) on 18th June 1940:

> ... the Battle of France is over, I expect that the Battle of Britain is about to begin. Upon this Battle depends the survival of Christian civilisation. Upon it depends our own British life, and the long continuity of our institutions and our Empire... Let us therefore brace ourselves to our duties, and so bear ourselves that, if the British Empire and its Commonwealth last for a thousand years, men will still say, "This was their finest hour."

The Battle was the first major military campaign in history to be fought entirely in the air.

This Monument commemorates the Allied airmen of the RAF, who took part in this vital WWII battle. The men are known as "The Few" from Churchill's famous speech of 20th August 1940:

> Never, in the field of human conflict, was so much owed by so many to so few.

(It also alludes to Shakespeare's famous speech in his play, Henry V: "*We few, we happy few, we band of brothers..*")

Nearly 3,000 British and Allied airmen took part in the Battle of Britain; twenty per cent of those who participated were from countries outside Britain (at least 14 different countries).

The most famous fighter planes used by the RAF in the Battle were the Hawker Hurricane and the Supermarine Spitfire. Although the Hurricanes were more numerous, the Spitfire attracted more attention and became the symbol of defiance during the Battle. Many of the Spitfires were purchased privately at a cost of £5,000 each by individuals, towns and organisations, and the planes were often named by the buyer (e.g., "Dogfighter" was bought by the Kennel Club). At the height of the Battle of Britain on 30th August 1940, 33 Squadrons of Hurricanes (709 aircraft in total) and 19 Squadrons of Spitfires (372 aircraft in total) faced the Luftwaffe.

The Luftwaffe were unable to succeed with their plan and the RAF won the Battle of Britain, which officially ended on 31st October 1940, when the British were confident that there would not be an invasion that year. However, in September 1940, hoping to destroy morale, Hitler had launched "the Blitz", another air campaign, aimed at economic and civilian targets in London and other cities. The Blitz finally ended on 10th May 1941.

Churchill, who had foreseen the importance of air defence since before WWI, always wanted to be in the thick of the action and - to the horror of his security staff - he regularly walked around the streets of Whitehall and Westminster inspecting bomb damage. He even climbed onto the rooftops of nearby buildings during bombing raids, and observed the action first-hand.

Directions: *Cross the road (Embankment) where it is safe, and directly opposite the Battle of Britain Monument (**10**) is a closed road. Enter the path running alongside this, on the right hand side. This path leads to to Whitehall. In the centre of the road is the Monument to the Women of WWII (**11**).*

11 THE MONUMENT TO THE WOMEN OF WWII

This Monument was unveiled in 2005 by Queen Elizabeth II, as part of the 60th anniversary commemorations of the end of WWII. Military helicopters flown by all-female crews flew past the memorial to mark the occasion.

Around the 22ft-high bronze sculpture are depicted seventeen individual sets of clothing and uniforms, which represent the hundreds of different jobs that women undertook in WWII, and then gave back to the returning men at the end of the War.

Notice: To your right are the three Statues of WWII heroes - Field Marshal Montgomery of Alamein ("*Monty*"), Field Marshal Alan Brooke and Field Marshal Slim.

Directions: *Directly opposite is No. 10 Downing Street (12).*

12 NO. 10 DOWNING STREET

This has been the official residence of the Prime Minister since 1735.

On 30th September 1938, the then Prime Minister, Neville Chamberlain, arrived here by limousine, after meeting Adolf Hitler in Munich. Chamberlain went straight inside and leaned out of the upstairs window, waving the famous Munich agreement, which he had made with Hitler and other leaders. As the crowds in the street below cheered, Chamberlain proclaimed that there was: "*Peace with honour*" and continued: "*I believe it is peace for our time.*"

However, within a year, Germany had invaded Poland. On Friday, 1st September 1939, Chamberlain invited Churchill to No. 10, asking him to join the War Cabinet of six members. At 11.15 am on Sunday, 3rd September 1939, Chamberlain made an announcement from the Cabinet Room of No. 10. He sombrely announced to the country that the final ultimatum, set at 9.00 am that morning, had expired and that the country was now at war with Germany. Churchill was immediately made First Lord of the Admiralty.

Eight months later Chamberlain resigned as Prime Minister and, on 10th May, 1940 King George VI asked Churchill to become War Prime Minister and to form a new War Government. That same day, Hitler invaded Holland, Belgium and Luxembourg.

On the night of the 11th May 1940, Churchill went to bed in the small hours, and later recalled that rather than feeling nervous at the burden of responsibility of his new post: "*I felt as if I were walking with destiny, and that all my past life had been but a preparation for this hour and for this trial.*"

Churchill and his wife, Clementine, moved into No. 10 Downing Street in June 1940.

Years later, on Tuesday, 8th May 1945, the German forces in Europe surrendered to the Allies. It was VE Day – Victory in Europe Day (which marked the end of WWII in Europe - Japan was defeated three months later, thereby officially ending WWII). Churchill lunched with King George VI and then broadcast his victory speech to the British people from No. 10 Downing Street at 3.00 pm in the afternoon. "*The German war is therefore at an end*". After the speech, he got into his car and was pushed, by cheering crowds, all the way to the House of Commons (**18**), where he repeated the speech.

Churchill left No. 10 when he resigned as Prime Minister in July 1945, after being defeated in the General Election. He returned again in November 1951 (aged 77 years), after becoming Prime Minister for a second time. Churchill resigned his position in April 1955, on the grounds of age. On the eve of his resignation, the Churchills held a party at the house, which was attended by Queen Elizabeth II (the sixth monarch Churchill had served under).

Directions: *Continue down Whitehall, on the left hand side, until you come to the Cenotaph, which is in the centre of the road (**13**)*

THE CENOTAPH

This simple pale monument was completed in 1920, to commemorate the dead of WWI, but today also commemorates the dead of all subsequent wars.

Inscribed with the words: "*To The Glorious Dead*" and including no religious symbols, it is adorned by the flags of the three services and the Merchant Navy. Every year, on Remembrance Day - the Sunday closest to 11th November (Armistice Day) - the Monarch and leading politicians lay wreaths of poppies on the Cenotaph, in remembrance of all those who have lost their lives in war.

Directions: *Continue, and on the left, at No. 48 Parliament Street, is the Red Lion Public House (14)*

THE RED LION PUBLIC HOUSE

The Red Lion Pub stands on the site of a medieval tavern, which was known in 1434 as the Hopping Hall. Centuries later, when the Pub had been renamed The Red Lion, a young Charles Dickens was a regular visitor. He described the kind-hearted Pub landlady as having an "*admiring as well as compassionate*" attitude towards himself.

Standing so close to Downing Street and the Houses of Parliament, the Pub was a common haunt for politicians and ministers. It proudly boasts that it has served every British Prime Minister (including Winston Churchill and Clement Atlee) up until Edward Heath in the 1970s. Pictures of polical scenes and figures (including Churchill) are displayed around the walls. The Pub is friendly and serves food, including hand-crafted shortcrust pastry pies.

Also, in a tradition dating back 150 years, the Pub has a division bell. When the bell is rung, it signifies that Members of the House of Commons or the House of Lords have eight minutes to return to their "*division lobby*" to cast their votes at the end of a debate. Tourists at the Pub have been known to mistake the ringing of the division bell for a fire alarm!

Directions: *Continue along on the left and, notice the last large building on the <u>right hand side</u> of the road, before you get to Parliament Square; this is HM Treasury (**15**).*

15 H M TREASURY

Today, this building contains HM Treasury but, during WWII, this building and its basements were utilised by the War Office. The building contained many war related government departments including the Air Ministry and the Churchill War Rooms (**25**), from which Churchill and his advisors led the war.

The Air Ministry was a department of the British Governent which existed from 1918 to 1964. It was created to be responsible for the formation and management of the Royal Air Force (RAF), which was founded in April 1918 and was under the political authority of the Secretary of State for Air. In January 1919, Churchill was appointed Secretary of State for War and Secretary of State for Air. Churchill was passionate about technology, and in particular aviation. During his time at the Air Ministry, Churchill built up this area of defence, as he foresaw its importance for the future. In the summer of 1919, he also began to retake flying lessons (which he had abandoned in 1914, after a near-fatal crash). However, after another near-fatal crash in the same year, he finally gave up on his attempts to qualify as a pilot. Churchill was likely to have been the first politician ever to learn to fly.

In July 1936, there was a complete reorganisation of the RAF. At this time, a new section called Fighter Command was created, with Air Chief Marshal Sir Hugh Dowding being appointed its Commander-in-Chief. When Churchill became Prime Minister in 1940, he formed the Ministry of Aircraft Production, which was to be responsible for aircraft production for the British forces.

Churchill put his long-standing political friend Lord Beaverbrook in charge of the new department. Under Beaverbrook's control, aircraft production was increased, so that although RAF Fighter Command had been outnumbered in July 1940, by October, it had more fighter planes than the Luftwaffe. This was crucial in the Battle of Britain (**10**) where Fighter Command went on to earn great fame.

Notice: This building has a balcony that overlooks Whitehall, surrounded by eight white columns.

On 8th May 1945, on the evening of VE Day, after making a historic radio broadcast, Churchill, the Prime Minister, spoke twice to the thousands of people who had gathered here to hear his victory speech. Churchill and some of his colleagues appeared on the balcony and Churchill addressed the vast celebrating crowds, saying:

> *God bless you all. This is your victory!*

To which, the crowd responded spontaneously: "*No – it is yours!*" and sang: "*For He's a Jolly Good Fellow.*" Churchill continued:

> *It is the victory of the cause of freedom in every land. In all our long history we have never seen a greater day than this. Everyone, man or woman, has done their best. Everyone has tried. Neither the long years, nor the dangers, nor the fierce attacks of the enemy, have in any way weakened the independent resolve of the British nation. God bless you all…*

Churchill returned to the balcony on the next evening, thanking the crowds:

> *… for never having failed in the long, monstrous days and in the long nights black as hell.*

Directions: *Continue a little further to Parliament Square and, opposite, is The Churchill Statue (**16**).*

16 THE CHURCHILL STATUE

Created by Ivor Roberts-Jones, this Statue in Parliament Square, was unveiled by Clementine, Churchill's wife, on 1st November 1973, eight years after Winston's death. It stands on the spot where, in the 1950's, Churchill had declared "*that is where my statue will go*". The cost of the statue was approximately £30,000.

Queen Elizabeth II attended the unveiling ceremony, along with many others, including the Queen Mother, the Prime Minister, four former Prime Ministers and four generations of the Churchill family. The band of the Royal Marines played some of Churchill's favorite tunes (including Gilbert and Sullivan) and the bells of St Margaret's Church (**20**) rang out.

Shortly after the outbreak of WWII, in September 1939, Parliament Square was covered with barbed wire which, it was hoped, would slow down any invading parachutists. Later, a fake W H Smith bookstall, which concealed a concrete machine gun post, was put up, and sandbags were piled up in the area where the Statue now stands. There was also an air raid shelter for up to 400 people in the middle of the Square.

Directions: *Cross the road. On the left is Big Ben (**17**) and then The Palace of Westminster, which contains the Houses of Parliament (**18**).*

17 BIG BEN

Although "Big Ben" is actually the nickname of the main bell (the Great Bell) of the Great Clock of Westminster, the name "Big Ben" is generally used today to refer to the whole clock tower. (Officially, the tower is called the Elizabeth Tower).

Like most of the famous monuments in London during WWII, Big Ben was not illuminated for most of the War – in the wartime blackout, the lights would have been a highly visible target, allowing the enemy bombers that used the River Thames to navigate, to easily identify Whitehall and Westminster. Londoners regarded Big Ben, which never missed a strike throughout the most devastating raids of the Blitz, as a symbol of their resistance. The tolling of Big Ben was heard at the beginning of WWII radio broadcasts.

On VE Day, Churchill broadcast to the Nation that Germany had unconditionally surrendered and that hostilities were to officially end at one minute after midnight that night. Churchill finished his speech with the words:

> *and the German war is therefore at an end….Advance Britannia…God Save the King.*

The very moment Churchill had finished this speech, the celebrations began. As darkness fell that evening, the lights of London were turned on for the first time in over five years, illuminating Big Ben and London's other iconic buildings.

Just before midnight, the London sky was lit up by hundreds of search lights, which had previously been used to target enemy bombers during the Blitz. And at midnight, silence fell as thousands gathered around Big Ben, eagerly awaiting the chimes of midnight, when the War in Europe would be over.

On 30th January 1965, the day of Winston Churchill's funeral, as a mark of respect, Big Ben remained silent from 9.45 am until midnight. (In April 2013, despite some controversy, Big Ben was also silenced for the duration of Margaret Thatcher's funeral.)

18 THE PALACE OF WESTMINSTER (THE HOUSES OF PARLIAMENT)

The two Houses of Parliament (**18**) (the House of Lords and the House of Commons) are contained within the Palace of Westminster, the present building having been completed in 1870, after the original medieval building was almost completely destroyed by a fire in 1834.

As a young man, Churchill frequently visited the House of Commons to listen to his father, Lord Randolph Churchill, who was a Member of Parliament. Churchill revered his father as a great statesman, even though his father often expressed his disappointment in his son. (When his father died in 1895, aged only 45, Churchill, who strongly felt that he was destined for great things, was left with the belief that he too would die young).

Winston Churchill first took his seat in Parliament, in the House of Commons, on 14th February 1901, as the Conservative Member for Oldham. (He had gained his seat in 1900 at his second attempt). According to '*the Morning Post*', Churchill's maiden speech, on 28th February, was listened to by an audience "*which very few new members have commanded.*" His mother was amongst those in the Ladies' Gallery. The Daily Express called his speech "*spellbinding.*"

In the 1930s, Churchill already recognised the danger of the rise of Hitler

and Nazi Germany. In 1930, during a meeting at the German Embassy (**31**), it was documented that Churchill was not convinced by Hitler's declarations that he had no intention of waging a war of aggression. Churchill wrote in his newspaper columns and spoke on the radio, at meetings and in Parliament, trying to alert the Government to the danger. In 1933, he gave a speech in the Commons warning the Government about the threat of German rearmament.

> *Those Germans are not looking for equal status. They are looking for weapons.*

The following year, in March, he also urged in the Commons that there should be increased spending on the RAF and stronger air defences and in November, he warned that Germany would reach parity in air strength in 1935.

Churchill, however, was a lone voice. It was felt that Churchill was being alarmist. Also, many people did not want to hear about a possible new war with Germany, as memories of WWI were still fresh in their minds and everyone was hoping for peace. Unfortunately, Churchill was proven to be right in his warnings.

After the outbreak of WWII, when King George VI asked Churchill to form a coalition war Government, Churchill came here on 13th May 1940 to ask, in his first speech as Prime Minister, for a vote of confidence in his new all-party Government. Churchill's speech to the House included these famous words:

> *I would say to the House, as I said to those who have joined this Government: 'I have nothing to offer but blood, toil, tears and sweat.*

He continued:

> *… You ask, what is our policy? I can say: It is to wage war, by sea, land and air, with all our might and with all the strength that God can give us; to wage war against a monstrous tyranny, never surpassed in the dark, lamentable catalogue of human crime. That is our policy. You ask, what is our aim? I can answer in one word: It is victory, victory at all costs, victory in spite of all terror, victory, however long and hard the road may be; for without victory, there is no survival. …*

During the War, Churchill made many of his great and famous rallying speeches to the British public in the House of Commons, including perhaps his most famous speech, on 4 June 1940, after Dunkirk and before the Battle of Britain:

> *We shall go on to the end, we shall fight in France, we shall fight on the seas and oceans, we shall fight with growing confidence and growing strength in the air, we shall defend our Island, whatever the cost may be, we shall fight on the beaches, we shall fight on the landing grounds, we shall fight in the fields and in the streets, we shall fight in the hills; we shall never surrender …*

The location of the Houses of Parliament, by the River Thames, made it an easily identifiable target for the German bombers (the building was, in fact, damaged by bombs fourteen times during WWII).

Unbelievably, according to the House of Commons' own archives, a munitions factory was set up in the vaults under the Houses of Parliament in 1943. By the following year, over 100 staff, including volunteers recruited from members of both Houses and general staff, worked part-time shifts assembling detonator holders and fuses, producing torque amplifiers for anti-aircraft guns and inspecting shell fuse parts.

Directions: Continue, with the Houses of Parliament on your left, and the rear of St Margaret's Church on your right. If you continue further (to near the Statue of Oliver Cromwell) you will arrive at the Cromwell Green Visitors' Entrance to the Houses of Parliament and Westminster Hall (**19**)

19 WESTMINSTER HALL

Built in 1099, this is one of the very few parts of the original Palace of Westminster to survive. The Hall is now used for major public ceremonies.

On 24th January 1965, two weeks after having a massive stroke, Churchill, died at his home at 28 Hyde Park Gate, Kensington, London. He was aged 90. It was the exact day that his father had died 70 years before. On 26th January, Churchill's body was brought to Westminster Hall, to lie-in-state, an honour normally reserved only for Monarchs. During the next three days and nights, over 300,000 people queued to file past the coffin, which was draped with the Union Jack, to pay their respects.

Churchill was given a state funeral, only the fourth ever to be held in the City (at that time), and a rare honour to be granted to a commoner. On 30th January, placed on a gun carriage, the coffin was borne in a solemn procession lasting one hour to St Paul's Cathedral. Crowds of up to one million silent people lined the streets. A 19-gun salute was fired from St James's Park; at the same time, the RAF staged a flyby of 16 fighter planes (including Spitfires and Hurricanes). As a sign of respect, American flags were lowered to half-mast, and Big Ben (**17**) was silenced. In a break with royal etiquette, the Queen attended the funeral and awaited the arrival of the coffin. General de Gaulle of France was amongst the three thousand mourners inside the Cathedral.

Churchill's body was buried in the churchyard of St Martin's Church in Bladon, Oxfordshire, less than one mile from his birthplace. It had been his wish that he should be buried here, next to his parents, and with an unobstructed view of Blenheim Palace, where he had been born. Only two wreaths were placed on Churchill's grave. The first was from his wife, the other from Queen Elizabeth II.

Only months before Churchill's death, his daughter, Mary, had written to him. "*In addition to the feelings a daughter has for a loving, generous father, I owe you what every Englishman, woman and child does – Liberty itself.*"

Directions: Return to St Margaret's Church. Cross the road at the lights, turn left and 30 m further along enter a passageway on the right, which leads down the side of St Margaret's Church (**20**) .

20 ST MARGARET'S CHURCH

Founded in the 12th Century, the present day Anglican Church dates from 1523 and has been the parish church of the House of Commons since 1614.

Winston Churchill and Clementine Hozier, a society beauty, married here on 12th September 1908, He was 33 and she 23. Churchill had proposed to Clementine in the lakeside Temple of Diana at Blenheim Palace in August. Clementine said it was his "*dominating charm and brilliancy*" which eventually won her over. Their marriage was to last 57 years, during which time they had five children.

In a glass case, to the right of the altar, is displayed a copy of the marriage register, signed by Churchill on that day. Churchill later wrote to his mother:

> *What a relief to have got that ceremony over! and so happily.*

St Margaret's was repeatedly damaged by enemy raids during WWII.

Directions: *On your left is Westminster Abbey (21).*

21 WESTMINSTER ABBEY

There is too much of interest inside Westminster Abbey, in which most British Monarchs have been crowned and in which many are buried, to mention everything here. However, for the purpose of this Walk, if you decide to enter the Abbey, the following are of most relevance:

Just inside the entrance of the Abbey, there is a black marble slab surrounded by red poppies. This is the Tomb of the Unknown Soldier. Erected in 1920, to commemorate the dead of WWI, it is now a memorial to the dead of both World Wars.

Nearby, between the Great West Door of the Abbey and the Tomb, is a memorial stone with the words "*Remember Winston Churchill*". This was unveiled by Queen Elizabeth II on 19th September 1965, at the Service to mark the 25th Anniversary of the Battle of Britain. Clementine would leave flowers at this memorial two

times each year, on the anniversary of her husband's birth and his death. When Clementine died in 1977, her daughter, Mary, continued the tradition.

President Franklin Roosevelt is commemorated with a wall tablet just above the Churchill memorial. This was unveiled by the then current Prime Minister (Clement Attlee), with Churchill and Mrs Roosevelt by his side, in 1948. (President Roosevelt had died in 1945, while still in office). Beneath the tablet are seven leather-bound books of remembrance to WWII victims.

Visit also the Royal Air Force (RAF) Chapel, the most dramatic of the side chapels, dedicated in 1947 to the 1,497 RAF men killed in action during the Battle of Britain. (See (**10**)). The memorial window includes the emblem and motto of the RAF and near the bottom is the famous quote from Shakespeare's Henry V: "*We few, we happy few, we band of brothers …*".

In the Cloisters, note the monument, which honours the submarine branch of the Royal Navy, the Commandos and members of the airborne forces and special air services, who died in WWII. Churchill unveiled this in 1948.

During WWII, over 60,000 sandbags were piled around the Abbey – both on the inside and outside, to protect the precious building and its contents.

Directions: *Continue along the path at the side of Westminster Abbey, leading away from St Margaret's Church. Exit the black iron gates, turn left and, next to the Abbey Bookshop, is No. 1 Sanctuary Buildings (**22**).*

22 NO. 1 SANCTUARY BUILDINGS

At the beginning of WWII, this was the National Headquarters of the British Union of Fascists (BUF).

Sir Oswald Mosley, the leader of the BUF, founded the organisation in 1932. Mosley, a rich baronet, former Labour Cabinet Minister and ex-Conservative MP, was very impressed by the achievements of the Fascist leader, Benito Mussolini in Italy. The BUF were often known as the "black shirts" due to the uniform members wore.

By 1934, the BUF had 40,000 members. The party became increasingly violent and anti-Semitic, often expressing its views by marches through Jewish

districts in London. In 1936, the BUF was forced to abandon an intended march in the East End of London in the famous "Battle of Cable Street", when they were confronted by demonstrators from Jewish, Communist and left-wing groups and locals. After the "Battle", Mosley made a speech to his supporters from an upstairs window here.

In 1936, Mosley married his mistress, Diana Guinness, after the death of his first wife. (Diana was one of the famous Mitford sisters, who were cousins of Clementine Churchill.) The couple were married in secret in Berlin at the home of Joseph Goebbels. Hitler, with whom the couple was in regular contact, was one of the guests. Diana's sister, Unity, was even closer to Hitler and was described in an MI5 file as being *"more Nazi than the Nazis"*.

Another notorious member of the BUF was American-born William Joyce, who was the BUF's Director of Propaganda. Joyce led the party towards anti-Semitism.

In 1939, just before the outbreak of WWII, Joyce (who did not want to fight against Hitler) moved to Germany. Joyce became a naturalised German the following year. Joyce got a job with German radio as an English language broadcaster and, throughout the War, he broadcast Nazi propaganda from Berlin to London. Joyce became known in Britain as "Lord Haw Haw" and was soon a hated figure. After the War, Joyce was found guilty of high treason (his British passport was still valid when he defected to Germany) and hanged at Wandsworth Prison on 3rd January 1946. He was the last person to be hanged in Britain for treason.

All Nazi spies, who were condemned to death in the UK during WWII, with the exception of Josef Jakobs, were executed by hanging at Wandsworth Prison or Pentonville Prison. Josef Jakobs was the last person to be executed in the Tower of London, where he was shot by an eight-man firing squad on 15th August 1941. He had been captured shortly after parachuting into the UK during the War. Having broken his ankle when he landed, he had to be tied to a chair for his execution.

Directions: Looking across this busy section of several roads, you will notice, opposite, a large building with a dome. Cross the roads using the traffic lights and the zebra crossing, and enter the road called Storey's Gate, which leads past the Queen Elizabeth Centre. The domed building on your left is the Methodist Central Hall (**23**).

23   THE METHODIST CENTRAL HALL

This building opened in 1912 and the Suffragettes, who were campaigning for votes for women, met here in 1914. When Churchill had been appointed Home Secretary in 1910, he was put in direct charge of putting down Suffragette activism.

In 1945, Winston Churchill addressed the Conservative Party Conference in the building's Great Hall. The Great Hall has also welcomed many other world figures, who have come to speak or to attend events, including Mahatma Gandhi (in 1932), General de Gaulle (in the early 1940s) and Dr Martin Luther King Jr. It also hosted the first ever meeting of the United Nations in 1946. Churchill and President Franklin D Roosevelt worked together to help found the United Nations.

Directions: *Continue a little further along Storey's Gate to the Westminster Arms Public House (**24**).*

24   THE WESTMINSTER ARMS PUBLIC HOUSE

The Westminster Arms Pub is in the heart of political London. The main bar is on the ground floor, and there is a restaurant upstairs and a wine bar in the basement. The Pub is a popular haunt for politicians, journalists and civil servants working at the nearby Houses of Parliament. This Pub also has a division bell in the bar so that Members of Parliament can dash back to the House in time for the vote!

Directions. *Continue along Storey's Gate, cross Birdcage Walk at the crossing and continue into Horse Guards Road, keeping on the right hand side, to Clive Steps, where you will find the Churchill War Rooms (**25**).*

25   THE CHURCHILL WAR ROOMS

This vast maze-like complex of underground rooms was the British Government's WWII headquarters. The Rooms were built under a modern and steel-framed block of Government Offices. Initially prepared in 1938, so that they could be used in the event of war, they were further strengthened by July 1940, because of the German bombing raids on London. A layer of concrete one metre thick was placed above the Rooms, which by the end of

WWII, covered more than three acres, and became known as "*the Bunker*". The Bunker became Churchill's main base from 21st October 1940 until the end of the War.

The most important and historic room in the Bunker is the sound-proofed Cabinet War Room, where the War Cabinet held meetings and where many strategic decisions were taken. The cloth-covered table is still there, as is Churchill's brown wooden chair. In the early days of the WWII, Churchill said:

> *This is the room from which I will direct the war, and if an invasion takes place, that's where I will sit – in that chair. And I will sit there until either the Germans are driven back – or they carry me out dead.*

The Central Map Room, where many maps still have marker pins stuck on them, is close by. Although the Churchill War Rooms were used primarily during the London Blitz, the Map Room remained in operation 24-hours a day until the end of the War. When Churchill was Prime Minister, he visited the Map Room every day he was in London to observe the fortunes of his forces during the War. In 1945, it was here that he watched the results of the election, in which he was to be defeated, come in. A room marked "Lavatory" was actually the Transatlantic Telephone Room, where Churchill made telephone calls to President Roosevelt.

Directions: *Immediately above the Churchill War Rooms, on the ground floor, was the No. 10 Annexe.*

25 THE NO. 10 ANNEXE

In 1940, it was clear that No. 10 Downing Street was not safe for the Prime Minister. As it was felt to be vital for public morale for the Prime Minister to remain in London, and there was not enough space in the Churchill War Rooms for the Churchill household, it was decided, therefore, to convert the offices immediately above the Churchill War Rooms into living apartments.

These apartments, which are on the ground floor, to the right of the building's entrance and which had an internal staircase to the War Rooms, became known as the No. 10 Annexe.

If you look to the right from the entrance of the War Rooms, you can see a set of six windows. These are the windows to the private apartments of Churchill. Steel shutters, which could be shut when an air raid began, were put onto the windows (you can still see the holes where they were fixed). A reinforced concrete outer wall, which can still be seen today, was also built to protect the building from bomb blasts.

The Churchills moved into the Annexe, on 16th September 1940, and Clementine had the family's private rooms decorated in her own style to make them more homely. It was here that Churchill actually worked and slept for most of the War. Many Cabinet meetings were held at the Annexe and it was here that Churchill made many great speeches. Churchill often took early morning walks, followed by his bodyguards, in St James's Park opposite.

Directions: *Continue along Horse Guards Road; on your right, you will notice (set back in a garden) the Statue of Lord Louis Mountbatten, the uncle of Prince Phillip, Duke of Edinburgh.*

During WWII, Churchill appointed Mountbatten Supreme Allied Commander, South East Asia Command. In 1979, Mountbatten, his grandson, and two others were killed by the IRA, who had placed a bomb in his fishing boat. [**Notice:** The fortified brick wall behind the Statue – this is the back garden of No. 10 Downing Street (**12**)].

Directions: *Continue along, and enter Horse Guards Parade, and you will see Admiralty House (**26**), which is the brown-bricked building on the far left of the Parade Ground.*

26　ADMIRALTY HOUSE

This four-storey building, of yellow brick, was used as the home of the First Lord of Admiralty from 1783 until 1964, and it is part of a larger structure called Admiralty Buildings.

Churchill held the position of First Lord of the Admiralty twice – the first time was from 1911 to 1915 (during which time his daughter Sarah was born at the House) and again in September 1939, when his family occupied the top two floors of the House. On 10th May 1940, however, Churchill was appointed Prime Minister, after Neville Chamberlain resigned. It was here that Churchill summoned all his Ministers on 13th May 1940 and told them:

> *I have nothing to offer but blood, toil, tears and sweat.*

A few hours later, he repeated these words in his famous speech in the House of Commons (**18**).

If you look up at the main windows of Admiralty House, you will see the window of the top floor room, which was once Churchill's private apartment. It was here that he wrote some of his great speeches of the early months of WWI and also some of the early WWII speeches, including his "*fight them on the beaches*" (delivered on 4th June 1940) speech.

Churchill later wrote that the years spent at Admiralty House were the "*happiest of my life*".

Notice: On the left hand side, on the edge of St James's Park – the Guard's Memorial, which commemorates the war dead from the Guards Divison and related units during WWI and from the Household Division in WWII and other conflicts since 1918. The Household Division guards the Sovereign and the Royal Palaces.

 Directions: *Continue along Horse Guards Road and, at the end, on the right corner, is the Admiralty Citadel (**27**).*

THE ADMIRALTY CITADEL 27

This concrete building, covered in ivy, was built in 1940 as a bomb–proof, communications centre for the Admiralty. Constructed to withstand even a direct hit from a 1,000 lb bomb, the building has very thick walls and foundations, which are reported to descend 9 m (30 ft).

During WWII, the Citadel was described as being crowded, with about one hundred men and women working inside – there was no daylight or sounds of the outside world, only the sound of people at work. Grass was grown on its roof to camouflage the building from the air. Churchill called it:

> *The vast monstrosity which weighs upon the Horse Guards Parade.*

and Londoners nicknamed it "*Lenin's Tomb*". The machine gun slits can still be seen in places. Today, the building is still used by the Ministry of Defence.

 Directions: *Continue a little futher and you have now arrived at The Mall (**28**).*

28 THE MALL

The processional route to Buckingham Palace, the home of the British Monarch. In 1936, King Edward VII abdicated and Prince Albert, Duke of York (Edward's younger brother), came to the throne as King George VI. During WWII, the King and his Queen, Elizabeth, refused to leave London and regularly made public appearances in areas, such as the East End, which had been heavily bombed during the Blitz

On 13th September 1940 a Luftwaffe pilot flew along The Mall and bombed Buckingham Palace, destroying the Royal Chapel. This was the incident, which led to the Queen saying that now that the Palace had been bombed too, she could "*look the East End in the face*." The Palace was bombed on several occasions during the War.

On 8th May 1945, (VE Day), The Mall was crowded with tens of thousands of excited people, celebrating Victory in Europe. The Royal Family stood on the Palace's central balcony, waving to the crowds. In a break with Royal protocol, Churchill later joined the Family on the balcony. The Princesses Elizabeth (in her Auxiliary Territorial Service – ATS - uniform) and Margaret slipped out unnoticed to join the celebrating crowds.

Directions: *This is the end of Stage No.1 of the Walk. If you wish to continue to Stage No. 2, please continue following the Directions, using Map No. 2 to guide you. Continue to follow the route from The Mall (**28**) by crossing the road to the opposite side of The Mall and going up the Duke of York Steps (**29**).*

If, however, you wish to find the nearest Underground Station, turn right, continue down the Mall (**28**), walking away from Buckingham Palace and into Trafalgar Square. You will then come to Charing Cross Underground Station.

FURTHER INFORMATION FOR THIS WALK

Please note that times are given as a guide only.

John Lobb (38)
http://www.johnlobbltd.co.uk/contact/contacthtm
Tel: 020 7930 3664
Email: enquiries@johnlobbltd.co.uk
Open: Mon-Fri: 09:00-17:30; Sat.: 09:00-16:30

Lock & Co. Hatters (39)
http://www.lockhatters.co.uk
Tel: 020 7930 8874
Email: shop@lockhatters.co.uk
Open: Mon.-Fri: 09:00–17:30; Sat 09:30–17:00;
Sun & Public Hols: Closed

Berry Bros & Rudd (40)
http://www.bbr.com
Tel: 0800 280 2440
Open: Mon-Fri: 10:00-21:00; Sat: 10:00-17:00;
Sun & Public Hols: Closed

Truefitt & Hill (42)
https://www.truefittandhill.co.uk
Tel: 020 7493 8496
Open: Mon–Fri: 08:30-17:30; Sat.: 08:30-17:00

James J Fox (44)
https://www.jjfox.co.uk
Tel: 020 7930 3787
Open: Mon-Wed & Fri: 09:30-20:00;
Thurs: 09:30-20:45; Sat: 09:30-17:00; Sun: Closed

Turnbull & Asser (49)
http://turnbullandasser.co.uk
Tel: 020 7808 3000
Open: Mon-Fri: 09:00–18:00; Sat: 09:30-18:00;
Sun: Closed

Paxton & Whitfield (50)
http://www.paxtonandwhitfield.co.uk
Tel: 020 7930 0259
Open: Mon-Sat: 09:30-18:00; Sun: 11:00-17:00

Harvie & Hudson (51)
http://www.harvieandhudson.com
Tel: 020 7839 3578
Open: Mon-Sat: 09:30-18:00; Sun: 12:00-17:00

St James's Church (52)
http://www.sjp.org.uk
Tel: 020 7734 4511
See website for details of services, free lunchtime recitals and evening concerts (charge for these).

Piccadilly Market
http://piccadilly-market.co.uk
Tel: 020 7292 4864 (Market Manager)
Open: Mon & Tues: 11:00-17:00 (Food);
Tues: 10:00-18:00 (Antiques & Collectables);
Wed-Sat: 10:00-18:00 (Arts & Crafts)

The Ritz Hotel (54)
https://www.theritzlondon.com
Tel: 020 7493 8181
"Afternoon Tea At The Ritz" served daily at the Palm Court at: 11:30, 13:30, 15:30, 17:30 and 19:30

MAP NO. 2

KEY

- **28** The Mall
- **29** Duke of York Steps
- **30** Giro's Tomb
- **31** No. 9 Carlton House Terrace
- **32** No. 4 Carlton Gardens
- **33** No. 2 Carlton Gardens
- **34** Statues of King George VI and Queen Elizabeth
- **35** No. 31 St James's Square
- **36** No. 4 St James's Square
- **37** No. 20 St James's Square
- **38** John Lobb
- **39** Lock & Co. Hatters
- **40** Berry Bros & Rudd
- **41** St James's Palace
- **42** Truefitt & Hill
- **43** No. 29 St James's Place
- **44** James J. Fox
- **45** 14 Ryders Court
- **46** Boodles Club
- **47** Cassini House
- **48** Jermyn Street
- **49** Turnbull & Asser
- **50** Paxton & Whitfield
- **51** Harvie & Hudson
- **52** St James's Church
- **53** The "Allies" Statue
- **54** The Ritz Hotel
- **55** Green Park Underground

The walk route

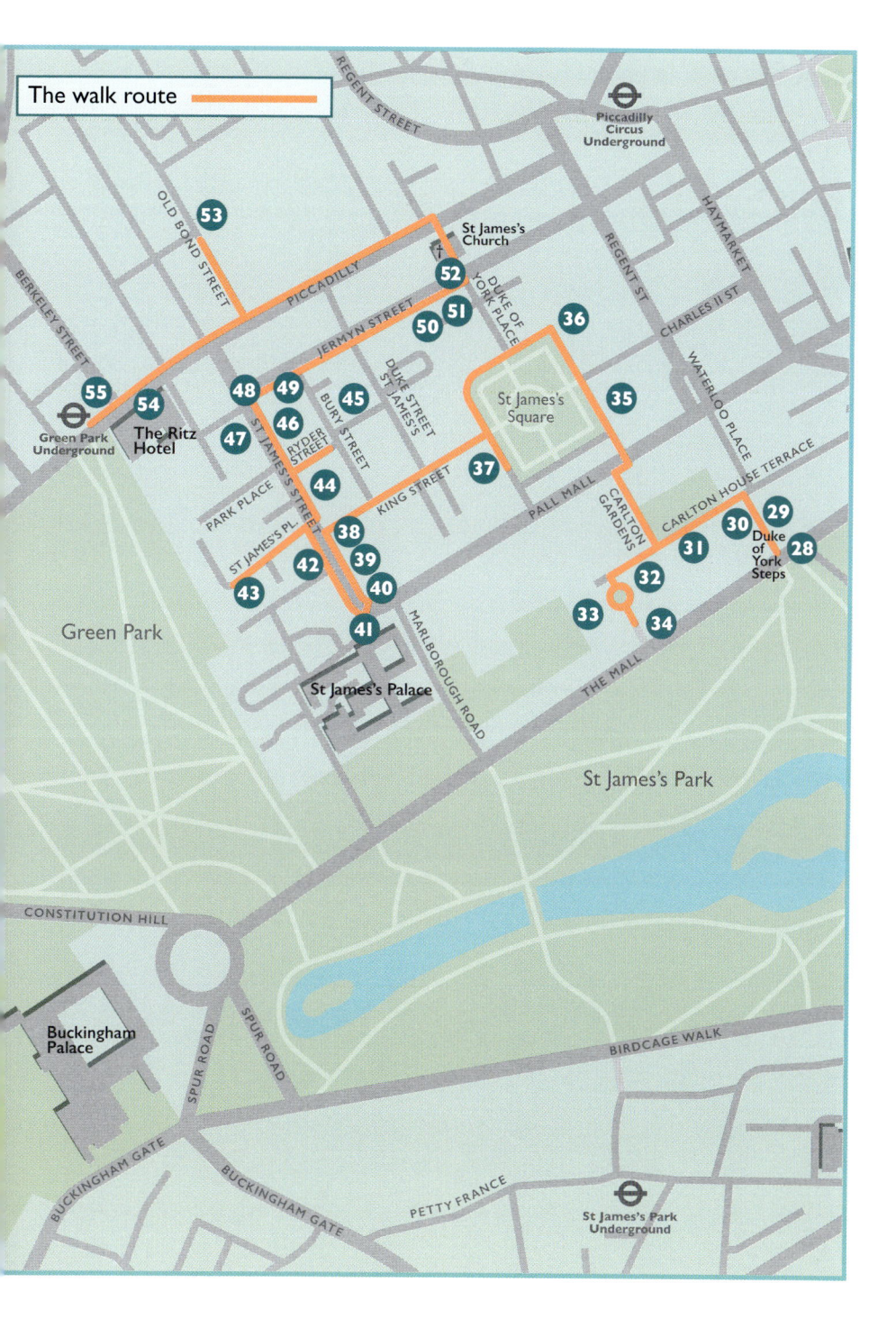

Map labels

- Piccadilly Circus Underground
- OLD BOND STREET
- REGENT STREET
- PICCADILLY
- St James's Church
- JERMYN STREET
- DUKE OF YORK PLACE
- REGENT ST
- CHARLES II ST
- HAYMARKET
- BERKELEY STREET
- DUKE STREET ST JAMES'S
- BURY STREET
- St James's Square
- WATERLOO PLACE
- Green Park Underground
- The Ritz Hotel
- PARK PLACE
- ST JAMES'S STREET
- RYDER STREET
- KING STREET
- PALL MALL
- CARLTON GARDENS
- CARLTON HOUSE TERRACE
- Duke of York Steps
- ST JAMES'S PL.
- Green Park
- St James's Palace
- MARLBOROUGH ROAD
- THE MALL
- St James's Park
- CONSTITUTION HILL
- Buckingham Palace
- SPUR ROAD
- BIRDCAGE WALK
- BUCKINGHAM GATE
- PETTY FRANCE
- St James's Park Underground

Route points: 28, 29, 30, 31, 32, 33, 34, 35, 36, 37, 38, 39, 40, 41, 42, 43, 44, 45, 46, 47, 48, 49, 50, 51, 52, 53, 54, 55

39

START OF STAGE NO. 2
Please Use Map No. 2

Directions: *Cross The Mall (**28**) at the traffic lights and walk up the Duke of York Steps (**29**). Enter Carlton House Terrace. Immediately at the top of the stairs, on your left, behind small black iron gates, is Giro's Tomb (**30**).*

30 — GIRO'S TOMB

This small monument, which is situated in an area which was once the front garden of No. 9 Carlton House Terrace, is the grave of Giro, the pet Alsatian dog of the German Ambassador from 1932-1936, Leopold Von Hoesch. Giro died in February 1934, when he chewed through a cable and was electrocuted. The small tombstone is inscribed with the words: "'*Giro: ein treuer begleiter!*" ("*Giro: a true companion!*"). Although Giro's owner was not a Nazi, this monument is regarded, by some, as the only Nazi memorial in London.

Directions: *Continue left a few steps, to No. 9 Carlton House Terrace (**31**).*

31 NO. 9 CARLTON HOUSE TERRACE (GERMAN EMBASSY)

This was the German Embassy from 1871-1939. The Ambassador from 1932-1936 was Leopold Von Hoesch, the master of Giro. Von Hoesch had become Ambassador when Germany was known as the Weimar Republic (1919-1933), before the rise of Hitler. Von Hoesch did not share the new Nazi political ideas and was worried about the increasing strain being put on Anglo-German relations. In 1936, he died here suddenly, aged only 55, apparently of a heart attack or stroke, although it was rumoured that the Nazis had assassinated him. Von Hoesch was regarded as the last representative of a pre-WWII democratic Germany and so the British Government gave him a full diplomatic funeral, with a 19-gun salute in St James's Park.

Von Hoesch's replacement was Joachim Von Ribbentrop, one of Hitler's favourites. Von Ribbentrop, helped by Albert Speer, Hitler's personal architect, began extensive and showy renovation work on the building and also on No. 7 and No. 8 Carlton House Terrace

Von Ribbentrop wanted to persuade the British Government not to interfere with German territorial disputes and to work with Germany against the Communist Government in the Soviet Union. Von Ribbentrop, however, was unpopular in London and did not help to improve Anglo-German relations. When he was presented to King George VI, on 5th February 1937, he greeted the King with a Nazi salute. He also stationed SS guards outside the German Embassy and flew swastika flags on official cars. In February 1938, Von Ribbentrop left to become Germany's Foreign Minister.

Von Ribbentrop (who was a great rival of Hermann Goering, the Air Minister in charge of the Luftwaffe), was arrested after the War and charged with war crimes in June 1945. He was found guilty at the Nuremberg War Crimes Trial and was the first of the war criminals to be hanged on 16th October 1946. (Goering had escaped justice by committing suicide with a cyanide pill).

Directions: *Continue along to No.4 Carlton Gardens (**32**).*

32 NO. 4 CARLTON GARDENS (HEADQUARTERS OF FRANCE LIBRE)

This was the headquarters of France Libre, the Free French Forces from 1940. The leader of the Free French Forces was General Charles de Gaulle.

In May 1940, German forces invaded France and reached Paris on 14th June. The French Government fled and organised French military resistance ended. General De Gaulle, a member of the French Cabinet, who, aged 49, was the youngest general in the French Army, opposed the Nazi occupation and surrender to Nazi Germany. When he saw that the new Government of France (centred in the town of Vichy) was about to surrender, De Gaulle was forced to flee to London. He wanted to continue the fight against the Germans and was able to secure Churchill's help. Thanks to Churchill, on 18th June 1940, De Gaulle was allowed to make a short, powerful and, now famous, speech, in French, to occupied France, on BBC Radio. He said: "*Whatever happens, the flame of the French resistance must not and shall not die.*" (During the War, General de Gaulle was to make over sixty such radio broadcasts.) The day after his speech, he was inundated with offers of help from French people, and, thus, De Gaulle set up France Libre (Free France), to continue the struggle against Germany, despite the fall of France.

Notice: The Plaque with the Cross of Lorraine (General De Gaulle's official symbol for Free France) and General De Gaulle's words.

When France surrendered to Germany on 22nd June 1940, the Nazis occupied three-fifths of France's territory leaving the rest to the Vichy Government. The Vichy Government, formally established in July 1940, under Henri Philippe Pétain, was a puppet regime, which collaborated with the Germans in the hope that they could still retain a measure of French sovereignty. Britain regarded the Vichy Government with suspicion and broke off diplomatic relations with it on 5th July 1940.

On 2nd August 1940, General de Gaulle was tried, in his absence, by a French military tribunal. He was sentenced to death as a traitor to France and his wealth was confiscated. When the public in London heard about this, people left jewellery, including wedding rings, on the steps of this building in support.

General de Gaulle was, apparently, a difficult character to work with and Churchill once said: "*Of all the crosses I have had to bear during this War, the* heaviest has been the Cross of Lorraine."

The Allied Forces, including France Libre, liberated France in 1944. On Armistice Day, 11th November 1944, Churchill was cheered as he accompanied General de Gaulle (now head of the provisional French Government) down the Champs Elysees in Paris.

Notice: The Statue of Charles De Gaulle a lttle further along the road, on the right hand side.

Directions: *Continue to No. 2 Carlton Gardens (**33**).*

33 NO. 2 CARLTON GARDENS (HOME OF FIELD MARSHAL EARL KITCHENER)

This was the home of WWI War Minister, Field Marshal Earl Kitchener, from 1914 to 1915. Kitchener devised the famous "*Your Country Needs You*" poster campaign here. The poster featured his own face and pointing finger.

Directions: *Walk past No. 2 and walk down the steps to appreciate the Statues of King George VI and Queen Elizabeth (**34**).*

34 STATUES OF KING GEORGE VI AND QUEEN ELIZABETH

Statues of the WWII Monarch (from 1936-1952) and the present Queen's father, and his Queen. King George VI was an unimposing, shy man, who never expected to, nor wanted to become King. However, the role was suddenly forced upon him, when his elder brother, who was King Edward VIII, abdicated in December 1936. King George VI reluctantly took the throne at a time when Britain was about to be tested to its limits.

The Royal Coronation of King George VI took place at Westminster Abbey on 12th May 1937. On 10th September 1940, regular Tuesday luncheon meetings between the new King and Churchill began and these continued throughout the War.

King George VI died on 6th February 1952 and his Queen, (who became known as Queen Elizabeth, the Queen Mother, after Queen Elizabeth II came to the throne) died, aged 101, on 30th March 2002 – they both lay in state in Westminster Hall (**19**) before being buried.

Churchill was very upset over the death of the King and paid tribute to him as a "*model*" sovereign in a radio broadcast he made the following day.

Directions: *Return to No. 4 Carlton Gardens (**32**) . Keep walking, and then turn first left into Carlton Gardens, which leads to Pall Mall. Cross the road at the zebra crossing and walk directly ahead into St James's Square. Stop outside No. 31 St James's Square, immediately on the right, which is Norfolk House (**35**).*

35 ▸ NO. 31 ST JAMES'S SQUARE (NORFOLK HOUSE)

The present Norfolk House was built in 1938. You will see two Plaques, which record the role, which the House played in WWII.

US General Dwight Eisenhower set up the Headquarters of the First Allied Forces here in 1942. The invasion of North Africa in November 1942 (Operation Torch) and the Allied invasion of north-west Europe in 1944 (Operation Overlord) were both planned at the House.

On D-Day, 6th June 1944, the first day of Operation Overlord, the Allies landed 156,000 troops in Normandy. It has been estimated that there were 10,000 Allied casualties (including 2,500 dead) on that day. The total number of German casualties is not known, but has been estimated as being between 4,000 and 9,000 men.

Secrecy was very important during the planning of the D-Day Landings – a private Staff bar was even set up at Norfolk House, so that Staff would not have to go to crowded public houses, where secrets could inadvertently slip out.

> The United States of America recognizes the selfless service and manifold contributions of General Dwight David Eisenhower, Supreme Allied Commander, 1944-1945. At this site, General Eisenhower, on behalf of freedom loving peoples throughout the World, directed the Allied Expeditionary Forces against Fortress Europe, 6 June 1944.
>
> This plaque was dedicated by a United States Department of Defense delegation and the Eisenhower family on 4 June 1990 during the Centennial year of his birth and the 46th Anniversary of Operation OVERLORD.

With this in mind, it is almost unbelievable that, a short time before D-Day, a man named Anthony Blunt (who was later revealed to be a Soviet Spy), got a job at Norfolk House, in a secret department, which ran the Deception Operation for D-Day. This important department helped to feed the Germans with disinformation about the date and locations of the Landings. It is thought by some that Blunt passed on true information about the movements of Allied troops in France to the Russian KGB, who in turn passed this information onto the Germans. This delayed the British/American advance, thereby enabling Russian troops (who were moving westwards) to reach Berlin first. Blunt helped to recruit others including Kim Philby (see (**45**)) Guy Burgess and Donald Maclean for the KGB at Cambridge University; together, they are the four known members of the so-called "Cambridge Spy Ring".

Directions: *Continue directly ahead to the corner, which is No. 4 St James Square; this was the Astor Family Home (**36**).*

36 NO. 4 ST JAMES'S SQUARE (ASTOR FAMILY HOME)

This house was built in 1728. Between 1912 and 1942, the wealthy Conservative politician, William Waldorf Astor II and his American wife, Nancy, lived here. Nancy had become interested in British politics, and she decided to try to stand for election, in order to win the seat. She won and in 1919, she became the first woman to take her seat in the House of Commons. In 1923, she became the first woman to introduce a bill into Parliament (the bill was to prohibit bars from selling alcohol to under-18s). She continued as an MP until 1945.

Nancy and her husband liked entertaining, and guests who visited this house included Gandhi, Charlie Chaplin, Charles Lindbergh and Joachim Van Ribbentrop (in 1936, just before he became German Ambassador) (see (**31**)).

Nancy Astor was known as a strong-willed, witty and outspoken woman. She is noted as saying: "*I married beneath me. All women do.*" Another of her famous quotes was: "*We are not asking for superiority for we have always had that; all we ask is equality*".

It seems that Churchill found Lady Astor rather annoying, and there were many documented verbal exchanges between the pair; one of the most famous is recorded as:

Lady Astor:

" *Winston, if I were your wife, I'd put poison in your coffee.* "

Churchill:

" *Nancy, if I were your husband, I'd drink it.* "

From 1943 to 1945, the building was used as a meeting place for Free France. It is now the home of the In & Out (Naval and Military Club).

Directions: *Continue walking around St James's Square and cross King Street. On the right is No. 20 St James's Square (**37**).*

37 ▸ NO. 20 ST JAMES'S SQUARE (HOME OF QUEEN ELIZABETH, THE QUEEN MOTHER)

This was the London home of Elizabeth Bowes-Lyon (later Queen Elizabeth, the Queen Mother – see (**34**)) from 1906 to 1920.

Directions: *Walk back to King Street and enter the Street. Continue to the end and turn left into St James's Street, stopping at No. 9, which is the Bootmakers, John Lobb (**38**).*

38 ▸ JOHN LOBB

Established in 1866, John Lobb, Bootmaker has served the Royal Family since the time of Edward, Prince of Wales (later to become King Edward VII) and the current Prince of Wales and the Duke of Edinburgh are customers today. Churchill bought his boots here.

[On 26th December 1941, when he was in the USA, having talks with President Roosevelt, Churchill had a slight heart attack. Although Churchill continued with his very heavy schedule, he was able to spend five days recuperating in Florida at the beginning of January 1942. His condition and movements were kept top secret. Churchill used the pseudonym "*Mr Lobb*" at this time. Although the Press guessed who he was, nothing was mentioned in the newspapers about it.]

Directions: *Continue to No. 6 James's Street, which is Lock & Co. Hatters (**39**).*

39 ▸ LOCK & CO. HATTERS

The world's oldest hat shop, whose famous customers have included: Admiral Lord Nelson, the Duke of Wellington (the plumed hat he wore at the Battle of Waterloo in 1815, came from this shop), Charlie Chaplin and Oscar Wilde. Today, the shop includes the patronage of Queen Elizabeth II.

Churchill was also a customer here, wearing a Lock silk top hat on his wedding day to Clementine Hozier in 1908, and in 1911, Churchill returned to the shop to order a white yachting cap, complete with the Royal Yacht Squadron badge. He was rarely seen without his signature "Homburg hat", which he also ordered from the shop.

Well-known for his extravagant, classically British, slightly eccentric and famously defiant personal style as much as his politics, Churchill commented that:

> *A gentleman buys his hats at Locks (**39**), his shoes at Lobbs (**38**), his shirts at Harvie and Hudson (**51**), his suits at Huntsman and his cheese at Paxton & Whitfield (**50**).*

Directions: *Continue to Berry Bros & Rudd at No. 3 (**40**).*

40 BERRY BROS & RUDD

Established in the 1690's, this is Britain's oldest wine and spirit merchant. It supplies the Royal Family. Inside, you will be able to purchase Pol Roger champagne, which is well known as having been Winston Churchill's favourite champagne. (Churchill had bought Pol Roger since 1908, and his favourite vintage was Pol Roger 1947). It was not easy to get champagne during WWII, but Churchill made sure that emergency supplies of Pol Roger were kept at the Churchill War Rooms (**25**). He remarked that: "*A glass of Champagne imparts a feeling of exhilaration. The nerves are braced; the imagination stirred, the wits become more nimble.*" In 1984, "*Pol Roger Cuvée Sir Winston Churchill*" was launched, named after its famous advocate.

Churchill's favourite whisky was Johnnie Walker Black Label. Churchill was so obsessed with this that when, in 1932, he painted a still life painting (he took up painting in 1915) called "*Bottlescape*", a bottle of this whisky clearly featured in it.

Directions: *Cross the road, using the two zebra crossings, to the gates of St James's Palace (**41**).*

41 ST JAMES'S PALACE

St James's Palace is not open to the public. To the right of the Gatehouse, with its clock tower and guard, is the Chapel Royal and then, further along, is the West Wing of the Palace, which is now called Lancaster House. King Edward VIII lived here before he came to the throne, when he was the Prince of Wales. In the mid-1930s, the Prince would secretly leave the Palace to meet his mistress, a married (her second marriage) American lady named Mrs Wallis Simpson.

When King Edward VIII came to the throne on the death of his father, King George V, in January 1936, he did not want to give up Mrs Simpson. However, as King and the Supreme Governor of the Church of England, Edward could not marry a divorcee. Edward was forced to choose between the Crown and the woman he loved.

During this time, known as "*the Abdication Crisis*", Churchill, who had known and been friends with the new King for at least twenty-five years, was amongst those who tried to persuade Mrs Simpson to give Edward up. However, on 2nd December, the affair became public knowledge and on 11th December

1936 Edward abdicated. Churchill incurred great unpopularity for his support of Edward during this time. Edward left London for Europe and in 1937, he married Wallis Simpson (who was now divorced) in France. The couple became the Duke and Duchess of Windsor.

Edward was never crowned King, and his reign had only lasted 325 days. He was the only British Monarch to resign from the position voluntarily. His younger brother Albert, became the new King, taking the title of King George VI (see (**34**)).

There was also another reason why Edward caused problems for his country: many felt that he and his wife were too sympathetic towards Nazi Germany. In 1937, Edward and his new wife (who had been friends with the German Ambassador Joachim von Ribbentrop (see (**31**)) visited Germany. There they met Hitler, and dined with his deputy, Rudolf Hess. In the summer of 1940, when France fell to the Nazi's, the Windsor's fled to Spain and then to Lisbon. It is said that the Nazis made contact with Edward and offered him fifty million Swiss Francs to go to Germany. If this had failed, their orders were to kidnap him. One theory was that Hitler wanted to reinstate Edward as King of England, when the Nazis won the War.

Churchill, who became Prime Minister in May 1940, was very concerned about the activities of the Windsors. He quickly made plans to move Edward to the Bahamas, a safe haven, where he was to be Governor. Edward and Wallis stayed there until 1945. Edward lived abroad until he died (in Paris) in 1972. Wallis died in 1986. It seemed that Churchill always had sympathy for Edward and, even when the Duke of Windsor died, Churchill tried to keep incriminating material about the Duke from being published.

Oswald Mosley (see (**22**)) married his first wife, Lady Cynthia Curzon, in the Chapel Royal in 1920 – it was said to have been the society event of the year. Guests included King George V and Queen Mary and other members of European Royal Families.

Directions: *Go back down St James's Street. On the left hand side, at No. 71, is Truefitt & Hill (**42**).*

42 TRUEFITT & HILL

Truefitt & Hill is a gentlemen's barber and perfumer. Established in 1805, it is recorded to be the oldest barbershop in the world, although the present location only dates from 1994. Truefitt & Hill was Winston Churchill's barbers, and its many famous clients include the present Duke of Edinburgh.

Directions: *Continue, and turn left into St James's Place. Near the end, on the left, is No. 29 St James's Place (**43**).*

NO. 29 ST JAMES'S PLACE (CHURCHILL'S CHILDHOOD HOME)

43

A Green Plaque honours Winston Churchill's childhood home (1880-1883). Churchill lived here as a young boy under the care of his nanny, Mrs Everest, before leaving to start his formal education at a number of boarding schools.

Churchill's parents were very active in society, but were distant from their children. Mrs Everest, who Churchill called "*Woom*" or "*Woomany*", (as he could not not manage to say "Woman"), provided Winston with the affection which his parents did not provide. In later years, Churchill wrote: "*My nurse was my confidante*" and "*Mrs Everest it was who looked after me and tended to all my wants. It was to her I poured out my many troubles*". Mrs Everest was employed by the Churchill family in early 1875, a few months after Winston's birth, and remained with them until 1893, when she was let go.

Notice: Spencer House at No. 27 St James's Place, which is the ancestral home to Princess Diana. Winston Churchill was a distant relation of Diana.

Directions: *Return to St James's Street. Notice, as you return, on the right hand side of the road, a small secretive courtyard, which leads to The Dukes Hotel.*

THE DUKES HOTEL AND THE DUKES BAR

Ian Fleming, author of the "James Bond" books, was regularly seen at the now legendary Hotel bar – the Dukes Bar. It is said to have been here that Ian Fleming gave Bond his passion for Martinis and invented the phrase "*shaken, not stirred*" following a discussion about the best way to make a Martini with the bar staff.

Winston Churchill, was a friend and fellow officer of Fleming's father, Valentine. They both served in the Queen's Own Oxfordshire Hussars during WWI. When Valentine was killed in France by a German bomb, Churchill wrote his obituary for The Times. Ian, who was aged just eight years old, was filled with admiration for Churchill and apparently framed Churchill's words and subsequently hung them in every house in which he lived. Ian Fleming continued to look up to Churchill and even went on to allude to Churchill as someone to be revered in his novel "From Russia, With Love" (1957).

Directions: *Walk back to St James's Street and cross the road at the zebra crossing. Turn left and, on your right at No. 19 St James's Street, is the Cigar Merchant, James J. Fox (**44**).*

44 ▶ JAMES J. FOX

One of the world's most famous and oldest cigar merchants, which has traded from these same premises for over 225 years. It has had many famous customers over the years, including Churchill and British and Foreign Royalty.

Apparently, the young Winston Churchill began his love affair with cigars in around 1895, when he travelled to Cuba to gather information, as a military observer, about the Spanish Army's fight against the Cuban guerillas. (Churchill began his career as a journalist by sending articles from Cuba to a London newspaper, called the Daily Graphic.) Although Churchill's mother, Lady Randolph Churchill, is said to have hated her son's habit of smoking cigars and had tried to make him give it up, it is said that she introduced Winston to this establishment. Churchill was a loyal customer for many years: opening an account at the shop on 9th August 1900, when he was a War Correspondent and continuing to be a customer until shortly before he died.

Churchill understood the strong image that smoking a cigar could project, and was rarely seen without his cigar. It is reputed that he smoked around 10 cigars a day, (or 250,000 during his lifetime), but rarely inhaled and never seemed to smoke them more than halfway. Churchill felt that there was a romance about a cigar and once wrote:

> *Smoking cigars is like falling in love. First you are attracted to its shape; you stay for its flavour, and you must always remember never, never to let the flame go out.*

Churchill's favourite cigar, which can still be purchased at the shop, was a Havana seven inch by 47-ring gauge Romeo Y Julieta. The brand commemorated Churchill's 1946 visit to Cuba, by placing his name on the cigar band of this size of cigar.

[The "Big Three" leaders of the Allied Powers - Churchill, Roosevelt and Stalin - all smoked. However, on the opposing Axis side, Mussolini and Hitler were non-smokers; and the first anti-smoking campaign was launched by the Nazis.]

Churchill placed his last order with the firm on 23rd December 1964, just a few weeks before his death. There is a very interesting small museum related to Churchill and cigars in the basement of the shop. Customers can sit in Churchill's favourite chair, and enjoy a fine smoke.

Another regular customer at the shop was Oscar Wilde. According to the shop's original handwritten ledgers, which you can see on display, the bankrupt Wilde left England owing the shop £37.17s.3d of unpaid bills.

Directions: *Continue along and turn right into Ryder Street, stopping at the junction with Bury Street. Across the road, on the opposite left hand corner, is No. 14 Ryder Court (**45**).*

45 NO. 14 RYDER COURT

During WWII, these offices were used by British MI6 and American intelligence officers. Kim Philby, the Soviet "*mole*", often worked late into the night here from 1943 to1944. He would set his colleagues' minds at rest by saying he would lock up their desks! Philby's scheming worked so well that he was put in charge of the new anti-Soviet section here. One of the American officers to work here was James Angleton, who later became a founder of the CIA.

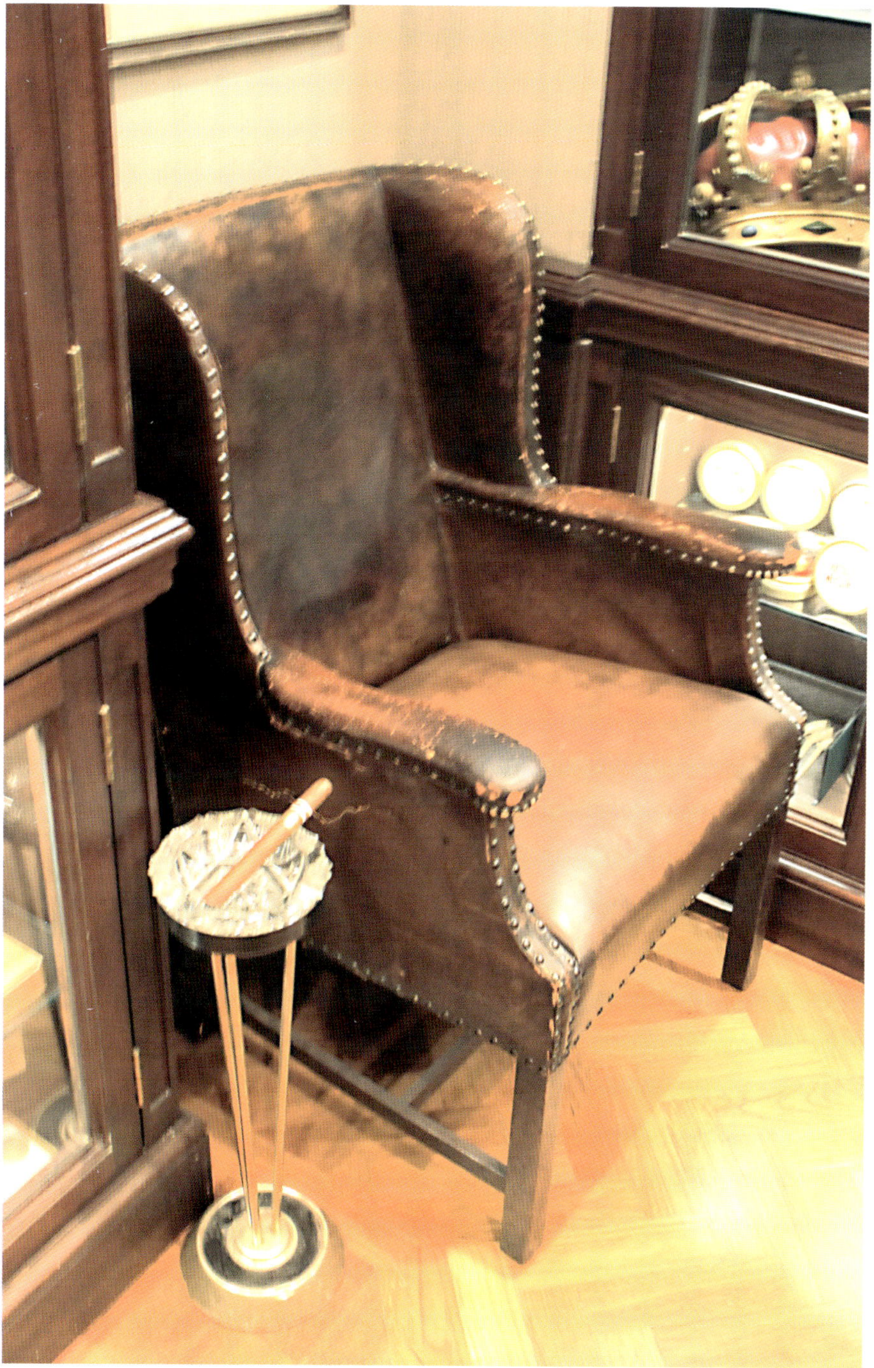

Directions: *Return to St James's Street and turn right and stop outside No. 28 St James's Street (**46**).*

46 BOODLE'S CLUB

Founded in 1762, originally as a coffee house, this is a social and non-political private club. It became famous for its gambling. Ian Fleming was a member here. He used Boodles as the model for "*Blades*", the club "*M*" (from the "James Bond" novels) is a member of. Churchill was an honorary member of Boodles.

Directions: *On the opposite side of the road, is Cassini House (at Nos 57-58 St James's Street (**47**).*

47 CASSINI HOUSE

During WWII, from 1940 to 1945, this building was the headquarters of MI5.

Among those working here was Victor Rothschild, millionaire member of the famous banking dynasty and scientist, who was involved in the race to develop atomic weapons before the Nazis. Rothschild was also the head of the unit, which organised the dismantling of bombs entering Britain. The Nazis hid devices in everyday items, such as boxes of chocolates and lumps of coal, and Rothschild once publicly made safe a bomb, which had been placed in a crate of onions! Rothschild was awarded the George Medal (created by King George VI in 1940) and made responsible for ensuring that "*gifts*" given to Churchill were safe. Churchill's appreciation of cigars, fine foods and drink made him vulnerable to assassination, therefore items such as cigars, hams, port and brandy bottles were tested to make sure they did not contain hidden bombs or poison. (In 1941, Churchill received a gift of 2,400 Havana cigars from the President of Cuba - one cigar from every box had to be tested for poison before Churchill could enjoy them.)

Directions: *Continue and turn right into Jermyn Street (**48**).*

48 JERMYN STREET

This Street was heavily bombed on the night of 16th April 1941. The raid, which started at 11.00 pm and lasted six hours, involved over 600 enemy bombers dropping approximately 900 tons of high explosive and 150,000 incendiary bombs over Central London. The raid was one of the heaviest of the London Blitz and over 1,000 Londoners were killed that night.

Directions: *Walk down the right hand side of Jermyn Street to Nos 71-72, Turnbull & Asser (**49**).*

49 — TURNBULL & ASSER

A gentleman's bespoke shirtmaker, clothier and tie maker, which was established in 1885. Churchill was also a customer here, where he was apparently known as a size 46, rather than the Prime Minister! The company's iconic shirts were a favourite of Churchill's and he wore them throughout his time in office.

Churchill was also famous for wearing a comfortable, practical one-piece boiler suit style garment, which could be slipped on over his ordinary clothes, and worn in air raid shelters when an air raid took place. Nick-named the "*Siren Suit*" by the House of Commons (or the "*Romper Suit*" as Churchill called it), it was oversized, made from tough wool and often featured a belted waist. Churchill liked the suit so much that he had versions made for himself in different designs and fabrics (such as pinstripe and a special velvet one with an added cigar pocket) and even wore these in meetings with people like Eisenhower and Montgomery.

An original green velvet edition of Churchill's Siren Suit is displayed behind a glass case at the store. To mark the 50th anniversary of Churchill's death, Turnbull and Asser recreated the Suit in either Elgin Donnegal 100% wool or 14oz navy wool fox flannel. The store also honoured Churchill with a special commemorative collection of men's accessories - containing a number of fine Churchill-inspired designs, including neckties, bowties, luggage sets and a series of pocket squares with a Churchill cartoon on them. So now, you too, can replicate Churchill's unique style!

James Bond wears bespoke shirts from Turnbull & Asser on screen and the store even created a special limited edition James Bond evening shirt for the film "Casino Royale" (2006).

Directions: *Continue to No. 93 Jermyn Street, which is Paxton & Whitfield (**50**). (Remembering Churchill's observation that: "A gentleman buys his hats at Locks (**39**), his shoes at Lobbs (**38**), his shirts at Harvie and Hudson (**51**), his suits at Huntsman and his cheese at Paxton and Whitfield (**50**) ")*.

50 — PAXTON & WHITFIELD

Paxton & Whitfield was established in 1797, and is one of the oldest cheesemongers in England. In 1850, they were appointed cheesemongers to Queen Victoria, the first of many Royal Warrants that the company has held over the years. Today they are Royal Warrant holders to the present day Queen and The Prince of Wales.

Churchill was a customer here and his favourite cheese was said to be Stilton (when he was in the trenches in 1916, he wrote to Clementine requesting:

"*large slabs of corned beef: Stilton cheeses: cream: ham: sardines – dried fruits: ...*") although he was also partial to Roquefort.

Directions: *Walk a little further to Harvie & Hudson, at Nos 96-97 (51).*

51 HARVIE & HUDSON

Shirtmakers and English outfitters since 1949, which was frequented by Churchill. Churchill enjoyed wearing bow ties and the shop supplies a "Churchill spot bow tie" – and a "Churchill spot silk handkerchief".

Directions: *On the opposite side of the road is the rear entrance to St James's Church (52). Enter the Church and walk through it. [If it is closed, use the side street nearby and walk to Piccadilly. Turn left and continue with the Directions.]*

52 ST JAMES'S CHURCH

Designed by Christopher Wren and consecrated in 1684. William Blake was baptised at the church in 1757.

On 14th October 1940, during the early stages of the Blitz, the Church was hit by high explosive and incendiary bombs. Fire raged and the Church was left as a burnt-out ruin. As the Rectory was destroyed, the Verger, Charles Murray and his wife, were trapped in the kitchen beneath. Rescue teams had to drill through large blocks of stone and masonry walls to reach them. Tragically, however, after being trapped beneath the rubble for over twelve hours, they both died of their injuries.

On the opposite side of the street (Piccadilly) another bomb made a massive bomb crater. A branch of the Fifty Shilling Tailors (a chain of shops selling men's clothes) was also set on fire after being hit by an incendiary bomb, causing molten wax tailors dummies to fall into the street. The nearby roofs of buildings glowed red with incendiary fires.

Although St James's Church was to remain roofless for almost seven years, services started again the following year under a temporary roof, and air raid shelters in the gardens were used.

Today the Church is well known for its musical concerts, and a thriving market (**the Piccadilly Market**) takes place in the Church courtyard six days a week.

Directions: *Exit the Church into the courtyard and cross Piccadilly at the lights. Turn left and continue. Turn right into Old Bond Street, continue down the street and, on the right on what becomes New Bond Street, is the "Allies" Statue (**53**).*

53 THE "ALLIES" STATUE

This bronze Statue, called "Allies", sculpted by Lawrence Holofcener, depicts Churchill (holding a cigar) and Franklin D Roosevelt sitting "talking" together on a park bench, and embodies the special relationship between the two men. The Statue was a gift from The Bond Street Association to commemorate 50 years of peace and was unveiled in May 1995.

In September 1939, President Franklin D Roosevelt wrote a personal letter to Churchill, who was at that time the First Lord of the Admiralty. Over the years, the pair exchanged nearly 2,000 messages. Churchill's mother (Lady Randolph Churchill) was American and, as well as he and Roosevelt becoming good friends, they were also distant cousins.

When WWII began in September 1939, President Roosevelt declared that the USA would remain neutral in law. However, he wanted to help countries who needed extra supplies to fight the Nazis. The UK, still reeling from its massive debts from WWI, needed financial help to buy military equipment and food supplies. Despite. President Roosevelt wanting to provide assistance, certain laws (the Neutrality Acts), the American military and also US public opinion (which was concerned that the USA would be drawn into the conflict). made things difficult.

The fall of France, in June 1940, left Britain in a desperate situation. Threatened with a Nazi invasion and with his country under savage attack, Churchill (now Prime Minister) was determined to obtain assistance from the USA and intensified his contacts with the President. As well as Roosevelt being personally sympathetic to Britain's cause, he also recognised that the interests of the USA were very much at stake.

In September 1940, President Roosevelt bypassed the Neutrality Acts, by developing a new initiative called the *"Destroyers for Bases"* agreement. In this, 50 US Navy destroyers were transferred to the Royal Navy in exchange for land rights on British possessions for the establishment of naval or air bases on **99 year rent-free leases**.

As well as helping the UK, the agreement was important for being the start of the wartime Anglo-American Alliance. Churchill said in Parliament that:

> these two great organisations of the English-speaking democracies, the British Empire and the United States, will have to be somewhat mixed up together in some of their affairs for mutual and general advantage.

After Churchill broadcast a now-famous speech over the BBC in February 1941 - which ended with an explicit heartfelt message to Roosevelt:

> Give us the tools, and we will finish the job.

- in March 1941, Roosevelt enacted a new initiative, named the "*Lend-Lease Act*". The act authorised the President to transfer arms or any other defense materials for which Congress appropriated money to "*the government of any country whose defense the President deems vital to the defense of the United States.*"

Roosevelt, eager to secure public consent for his controversial plan, had explained to the American people that it was comparable to one neighbour lending another neighbour a garden hose, to help him to put out a fire in his house.

By allowing the President to transfer war material to Britain without payment, the act enabled the British to keep fighting until events led America into the conflict. It also avoided the problems of war debts which had followed WWI. Britain, as well as the Soviet Union and other nations, received weapons under this law. In total, the USA gave away approximately $50 billion in military aid in

1941-45 (during WWII) - approximately $31 billion of which went to Britain - so that the Allies could better fight Nazi Germany and Japan. There was no repayment required. The Lend-Lease Act formally ended the semblance of neutrality by the USA.

The goodwill and respect engendered between the British and American peoples and governments during WWII was symbolised by the close personal and enduring relationship between Roosevelt and Churchill. In a speech made in the USA in 1946, Churchill spoke about how a *"Special Relationship"* had developed between the two nations. The term *"Special Relationship"* is now used to characterise the exceptionally close political, diplomatic, cultural, economic, military and historical relations between the USA and the UK – the existence of which has been recognised since the 19th Century.

In April 1963, Churchill was made an Honorary American citizen. He is only one of eight people who have received this honour (Churchill and Mother Teresa are the only ones of the eight who received this in their lifetimes).

As well as capturing the warmth of the relationship between the two great men, the *"Allies"* is very popular as it lets you sit between two of the 20th Century's most famous leaders.

Directions: *Go back to Piccadilly, turn right and continue to the Ritz Hotel (**54**), which is on the other side of the road and is followed shortly afterwards by Green Park Underground Station (**55**).*

54 THE RITZ HOTEL

During WWII, the Ritz Hotel was considered to be fairly resistant to the German bombs: The building had a steel frame and a basement air raid shelter. Also, the top two floors of the hotel were closed off (in case of a hit by a bomb) and the doorman stood by sandbags at the entrance. As a result, society figures continued to stay here and it was *"the place"* to be seen for dinner. In addition to figures from several European Royal Families, guests included Winston Churchill and his son, Nancy Mitford, General de Gaulle and Louis Mountbatten. Also, during this time, Churchill, General de Gaulle and Eisenhower met for summit meetings in the Marie Antoinette Suite of the Hotel.

If you want to enjoy a quintessential British experience, you can enjoy *"Afternoon Tea at the Ritz"* at the Hotel's Palm Court.

55 GREEN PARK UNDERGROUND STATION

There are public toilets here.
This is the End of the Walk.

CONTACT

Mr Paul Garner at *Louis' London Walks*

Email: llw@blueyonder.co.uk
Telephone: 07050 224991

LEGAL DISCLAIMER

This publication is an independent self-guided tour. Published in 2016, by Louis' London Walks. All the information contained inside this publication was believed to be correct at the time of going to press. Louis' London Walks can take no responsibility for any errors, or for any changes in times or other changes beyond our control that may occur. While every effort has been made to ensure your enjoyment and safety, the author and Louis' London Walks cannot accept responsibility for any accidents or consequences resulting from the use of this publication or from any errors found within.

Copyright © 2016 Paul Garner

All rights reserved. No part of this publication may be reproduced, stored or transmitted, in any form or by any means electronic, mechanical, photocopying, recording, or otherwise, without the prior permission of Paul Garner

© istockphoto pages 26, 30